A Letter To My Wife

A Letter To My Wife

JOSEPH DINARDO

A Letter To Marcia

My dearest love,

I write this letter tonight on tear-stained paper. My heart lies in pieces on our bedroom floor. But I want to share something with you before you go on your journey.

How or why this happened, I don't know. What I do know is that I love you so desperately that the thought of you not lying next to me ever again is almost too painful to consider. Watching you suffer and endure one treatment after another, seeing you ravaged and unable to eat for months, it was the hardest thing I have ever done. But nothing compared to what you went through, my love. I know that.

And I knew this day would come, though you never allowed me to really believe it. I begged and prayed that you would never leave me; yet, here I am, holding your hand, surrounded by family, and you, slowly slipping away, breath by breath. How do you look so beautiful, even as you start to drift away? I kneel before you asking for one last sign that you're okay. But you're not here, and, oh, how my heart breaks into pieces.

I remember two years ago when you were admitted to the hospital for what everyone thought was a simple scope to "snip" out a gallstone, and maybe to put in a small stent. Well, they did the stent, but the doctor said he did not see any gallstones and that your gall bladder was fine.

"Then what caused the blockage?" I asked.

"A growth on the pancreas seemed to be pushing a duct closed, Causing all the pain and backup," he replied.

"What do you mean, a growth?"

"I mean that I can't help you, and that you need to change your treatment options."

"What are you saying?"

"I am saying you need to go to Roswell."

I knew he meant Roswell Park Cancer Institute. It stung to hear.

"What? Are you saying my wife has a cancerous tumor on her pancreas?"

"I am saying you should go to Roswell."

Jerk.

I saw your face go white and your eyes tear for a moment. In that instant I had two overwhelming feelings. First, the fear and sadness of what this meant for you, for us. But at the same moment I was completely awash with the most incredible sense of love for you. Pure, unconditional love. I knew then that I wanted to, and would, be there with you for every step of this journey, wherever it may lead. I never knew how much I loved you and in that moment it rushed over me, a love I'd never shared or experienced before.

Thank you, my sweet.

Know this: Julianna, our daughter, is going to be okay. You have skillfully built a wonderful village around her with Hayley, Erin, and Mona, all her cousins and, of course, family and friends. We will all protect her and guide her and let her know she is loved and accepted in this world.

Your family is going to be okay. What a fierce protector you were for them. How you loved them all. I am so happy that in your final moments they were there right beside us, united in saying farewell to the daughter, sister, and aunt they loved.

Your mom, she will be okay. I know the thought of her burying her young husband and now her even younger daughter caused you such distress. But all of us will care for her, so please do not worry.

Me? We promised each other that we would always tell the truth, so no lies now.

I am not okay and never will be okay.

Okay is coming home from work, lying on the couch with a glass of wine, and watching you glide around the kitchen working your magic, preparing dinner.

Okay is going out to Hutch's or Giancarlo's for dinner and just talking and sharing for hours.

Okay is taking one of our trips—to Naples or another far-off city you scouted—with the whole family, or with our dear friends Chris and Andrea.

Okay is holding each other in an eternal embrace, loving so hard that tears flow from our eyes.

Okay is you here with me—that is okay. So I am not okay, but I will be here for Julianna, our vast array of friends, and our families. And I will be fine.

Maya Angelou wrote, "They will never remember what you said. They will never remember what you did. But they will always remember how you made them feel."

Oh, Marcia, how you made us all feel: your smile, your sparkling eyes, your pure pleasure in family and friends. You made each and every person that knew you feel a real connection, genuine affection, and true acceptance without judgment. Your posse of girlfriends near and far, I marveled at how you made every friend feel so loved, how you reminded each one that she had a special bond with you. I'll never know how you did it and they will each miss you so in their own way.

As for your nieces and nephews, how happy you made them feel each time they were with you—special, my love. You made them feel so special.

Marcia and I loved this song:

"Should I Fall Behind"
Bruce Springsteen

We said we'd walk together, baby come what may
That come the twilight, should we lose our way
If as we're walking a hand should slip free
I'll wait for you
Should I fall behind
Wait for me.

Well, your hand has slipped free. So go, and if it takes 10,000 years I will find you again. Have no fear as you travel. You are slipping away now—I see it and I know it. Holding your hand is the greatest privilege of my life. Thank you.

Now go, sweetheart. Your work is done here. Your suffering is soon over. Take as much of me as you want as you embark upon your journey.

Your devoted and loving husband,
Joe

Preface

I write this book to honor Marcia, her courage, and unique talent to love and be loved by so many. If I fail in this goal it is because I am a novice at writing anything longer that a college term paper or legal brief. But I will try my best nonetheless.

During the two years following Marcia's diagnosis of stage IV pancreatic cancer, a wide group of family, extended family, and friends circled around and showered us with love and emotional support. Novenas were said, masses performed, rosary groups formed, notes placed in the wall of the great Temple in Jerusalem, and so many loving-kindness meditations led. We received what felt like endless notes and cards, all of which I credit to keeping her alive just as much as the excellent medical treatment she received from Dr. Iyer and the Roswell team. But despite her valiant efforts, Marcia succumbed to the disease, and died on March 3, 2015.

When the funeral was arranged it fell to me to choose who would give the eulogy. I had been writing *A Letter To My Wife* as a personal and private final good-bye. I felt nothing and no one could truly do Marcia's life justice, but the letter seemed a perfect way to honor her. Afterward, so many people told me how moved they were by the letter that the idea for this little book began to percolate in my head. That is when I sought out Amy Koppelman, who, in turn, led me to my editor on this project, Yona Zeldis McDonough.

Transcribing what occurred during this time was a very emotional experience. Thinking it through brought those deep feelings of sadness and loss so close. But it was also helpful, and part of the ongoing process that grief requires. Amy, Yona, and I thought someone facing a similar situation might benefit from my sharing this story. I hope so. Even if it does not, I am still happy I undertook this transformational project and I would recommend the process to anyone dealing with grief following the loss of a loved one.

In this book, I am going to write about Marcia: the kind of person she was, what she means to me, and all the qualities that made her special. Then I am going to share how we came to be together, what I learned about love from being with her, and how she changed my life—forever.

Much love and thanks to Harper Spero who took over all social media aspects and assisted with anything and everything else that had to do with my book. William Gladstone, my whirlwind agent from L.A., skillfully guided us through Amazon and all the benefits that has provided. And Abby Bergman, Bill's assistant, a workhorse in every way.

Marcia's Magic

Marcia was the middle child of five siblings. Her father was a hard-working, blue-collar guy, a really solid person. He started out with a wheelbarrow and built one of the largest site contracting and paving companies in western New York.

Marcia grew up in Clarence, a Buffalo suburb. Even as a girl, she was always the star. No matter what she did or where she attended school, she always rose to the top. She had the best grades, the best friends, was the captain of her sports teams, and the prettiest girl around. But when I met her, she seemed unfazed by all of that; she was not self-centered or arrogant in any way. She grew up with two brothers and two sisters, and she was comfortable around cars, big equipment, and construction. She had a sense she was special but, amazingly, she didn't seem to care. She was grounded and approachable, yet she had such noble boundaries.

Marcia was also fiercely loyal to her family and close friends. She was like a mother bear with her cubs and no one could penetrate the powerful circle of love and protection she extended. The only hope you had was to try to become one of them. She let me do that from the moment we met.

Always a hard worker, just like her father, Marcia seemed to give more than was expected. She *loved* people and she loved social-izing. Dinner with family and friends was something she always enjoyed. And we enjoyed doing it together. She could go toe-to-toe with me in one-liners or storytelling—mostly stories about us—and we made such good-hearted fun of each other that I could tell people loved it—and her in particular.

Marcia had gone only to community college, so she was not formally educated. But you would not know that to speak with her. She navigated this world by intuition. She always said, "I know within minutes of meeting someone if she or he is someone I trust or want to be friends with." She was open and loving, but she was also able to tell people hard truths about themselves in a way that was always appreciated.

And though men were attracted to her, I never felt threatened or jealous because she was so loyal and made me feel so loved. I think I reminded her of her father in many ways and she knew she could trust me to support her in any challenge she might face. She had a wide circle of friends and I always marveled how so many of them felt that she was their best friend. She was able to always make each friend feel loved and accepted; when they got together, she focused only on them. It was a beautiful thing to watch.

She loved her wine but never drank too much. Tequila, however, was her passion. When with her girlfriends, often Marcia would call for one or two shots just for fun. She used to laugh freely as we playfully verbally sparred with each other.

Oh, how she loved life, and she lived it so fully.

A Match Made In Heaven

From the very first time I met Marcia—we had a lunch date—I was in love. She was beautiful, smart, and playful. We had an immediate chemistry and though she was flirtatious, I sensed that it was always within boundaries. We shared a common cultural background—we both had blue-collar dads and came from working class Italian families in western New York state.

Marcia fell for me as quickly as I fell for her. We could not keep our hands off of each other for very long. Our first trip to New York City together was like heaven, though getting her to join me there was not easy. I had told her how I often went to New York on business, and when I described the restaurants, shopping opportunities, and cultural events I could tell she was interested. So, the next time I had to take a trip I invited her to fly down. She agreed, but when I got to the airport to meet her plane, she was not on it. I tried again, with the same result. But the third time was the charm. When I watched her get off the plane, I could not believe that this beautiful, classy lady was actually on her way to meet *me*. And the fact that it had taken me three times to persuade her to come made the situation even that much more intriguing.

We first walked along Fifth Avenue to the Metropolitan Museum of Art, then we walked back down Madison Avenue toward the Pierre Hotel at 60th Street. We stopped for a cappuccino on the way. It was spring and everything seemed full of hope and joy.

Once back at the hotel, we had the courage to go to "our rooms." We made small talk for a little while and when we finally kissed the world exploded inside me. I could have made love for ten hours. I think we did. Everything about her was just so enjoyable. Her skin, her body, the smell of every part of her made me more and more wild. I could tell she felt the same way. I knew I was never letting this go. Anything she wanted, whatever I needed to do to make it right, I was going to do.

My body is in shivers just writing this. To think it has been more than two years since I was able to hold her tightly, kiss her freely, and make love to her again and again is almost too much to think about. Now the tears flow, the sobs come. Can they hear me in the other parts of this office? I don't care. I can't always control it. From the first time Marcia and I made love, it was like nothing either one of us had ever experienced before. And the most wonderful and extraordinary part of it was that it was like that *every* time for 20 years. The passion, the warm kisses, and our bodies moving like they were one.

And I so remember the last time we ever made love. You were between chemo treatments very early on and one night, when we were feeling particularly close, you wanted to make love—to my total surprise. I still do not know how you managed it. It was so wonderful, so warm, and you were so open and inviting.

As we finished, we both suddenly began to weep uncontrollably. We both seemed to know that that may have been the last time and that the journey we were embarking on had only one irreversible ending. As it turned out, it was the last time. I have never felt closer to a person than I did in those moments. How did you do that? Or, how did we do that? As I write I am once again open to those feelings and can touch that experience once more.

There was a time early in our relationship, before Marcia got sick, When we had gone to New York City together. After a great

4

dinner and a bottle of wine, we went back to the hotel, a little tipsy, and fell into bed, passionately in love. We rolled and enmeshed ourselves so deeply. Then, all of a sudden, we felt like we were in the air, coupled together and floating before falling gently to the floor. We laughed so hard yet we both had the same experience. I just don't know how it happened.

The pain of losing you has not diminished, Marcia; I have only learned to adjust to it. I practice just being here, exploring the depth and richness of these memories. I still feel you coming home. Or walking down the stairs in the morning as I am sipping coffee on the couch, waiting for you. But you never come anymore, just your memory, just the thought of you. Like a passing cloud across a blue sky, and then gone. Oh, I miss you so much. Without Julianna, I'm not sure what I might be or where I might go. Maybe I would disappear into our beloved Insight Meditation Center for a few months. But our daughter needs me, and so I remain rooted to where I am.

Marcia In The Kitchen

All of the Anastasi women are great cooks, but Marcia was the very best of them all. She knew everything about cooking—ingredients, condiments, methods, equipment. She never followed a recipe exactly, but preferred to work from intuition, always changing a little something here or there. I've enjoyed hundreds of meals Marcia made and, truly, there never was a bad one.

Marcia was on the cutting-edge of the farm-to-table movement, always traveling to different markets, selecting the best produce from one and the best meat, fish, or bread from another. When she and I discovered Eataly in New York City she thought she was in food heaven, and promptly filled a suitcase with delicious ingredients and groceries that she brought home to our kitchen. Of course she knew exactly what to do with them.

For 20 years I had the privilege and delight of watching Marcia prepare our nightly meals. I'd get home from work and sit down with a glass of wine, amazed at how she moved—or flowed, really—around the kitchen like a dancer, stirring this, tasting that. She would have multiple burners going and something cooling in the sink, but she made it all appear so effortless, sipping wine and talking as she worked. I am not a cook nor foodie, yet I loved to be included in Marcia's process to experience her creative, nurturing spirit in the kitchen.

During these lonely times, I wish I had paid more attention to it all, and to her. I now see how precious those moments were, and I miss them still.

A Woman of Grace, Beauty, and Style

To use a golf phrase, my wife was a "scratch" shopper. No handicap at all. Somehow she followed all the fashion trends and she always Knew what styles were hot, even before they became hot. She loved walking along Madison Avenue, especially in the spring and fall. She called it Adult Disneyland. She didn't waste money on just anything though, and what she bought always worked with what she already had. It didn't hurt that she was beautiful and filled out a designer's vision just the way they might have planned it.

She was five-foot-five with blonde hair and a face that was both outwardly beautiful and radiated her inner beauty. Salespeople loved working with her. She immediately charmed them with her warmth and jokes and easy laughter. She was never condescending or disrespectful. When clothes were delivered or sent to our home, the notes that came from the sales clerks were always sweet and thankful; these people always looked forward to seeing Marcia again. Armani was a special favorite—she loved both the fine fabric and the unerring fit. The service didn't hurt either. Everyone in the shop knew her and I could see that they genuinely enjoyed her company, even if she didn't buy a thing.

When she was done with Madison Avenue, Marcia would head over to Fifth Avenue for a stroll, making her way from Bergdorf Goodman to Saks, stopping everywhere in between. When she returned to our room, she would always be so energized. Whether she was alone or with a friend it didn't matter, she just enjoyed it all so much.

I remember our last trip to Naples, Florida. My beautiful, vibrant wife was nearing the end, at least that was how I saw it, and we had pretty much ticked off all the items on her bucket list, though only the two of us used that term. She was quite weak, and weighed less than 95 pounds. Yet, despite her condition, she insisted on taking Julianna and the girls on an afternoon shopping trip. I think she knew it might be her last. When they came home four hours later, Marcia walked in and went straight to bed. She was exhausted and barely alive but so happy to have spent the day as she did. Last in was Erin, our longtime nanny and close friend, carrying what looked to be 40 outfits on hangers and in plastic bags.

"What's all this?" I asked.

"Your wife felt she needed some new clothes that would fit." She was smiling but weeping a little, too.

"Erin, don't unpack them because I think we'll be returning them tomorrow."

Marcia never wore those clothes. She never really made it out of the bed. We took her home, back to New York, and a few days later we lost her.

Early Days: Joe

Being the child of an alcoholic poses a great many problems. Some of these are obvious, others, not so much. I don't know if it's because I had an alcoholic parent, but the reality for me is that I do not remember large segments of my youth. I do remember some events, and of course some of the characters that came and went. While I always thought that I was happy as a kid, I am now not so sure. I know that I harbored a mountain of anger that was mostly under control, but when it got out of control it scared me, and I did some things that make me cringe today.

There were four children in my family and we were very poor. My mother's father, Emilio Mascerelli, immigrated to the US through Ellis Island in 1911. He was just a young man at the time. He had a nice voice and clung to a dream that he might one day become an opera singer. But that didn't happen.

Nick Carbone, who was from my grandfather's home in Villamagna, Abruzzi, lived in Syracuse, New York. Nick had used a family priest to help kidnap a young girl from his hometown. The priest married them and he then took her to America. They settled in Syracuse and began a family. He was apparently quite difficult and mean-spirited. He treated his wife, Margaret, very badly. Well, Emilio asked if he could take a room with them until he was more settled and they agreed to let him.

Over the course of time Emilio and Margaret fell in love and decided to run away together. She left her husband and young family behind in Syracuse and they went to Cleveland. Somehow she had her marriage to Nick annulled and successfully married Emilio. They had three girls: Anna, Bertha (my mother), and Dina. They later settled in Rochester, New York. There, my grandfather, Emilio, became a coal truck driver and delivered coal to all the homes that had coal furnaces. He bought a house on Reliance Street to raise his family. Anna, his eldest daughter, met and married Horace Gioia, the son of a businessman who ran a successful pasta company. Dina, the youngest, married a chef who did quite well. Bertha married Carmen DiNardo in 1946 and I was born in 1947.

My father seemed to have been an alcoholic his entire life. A happy one. Not nasty or violent. And so his alcoholism went largely unnoticed or perhaps just tolerated, especially since he had served in the army in WWII and then had a job, albeit a low paying one, in a lumber yard.

We were four kids sharing a small fourth floor walk-up apartment—with mice, rats, or both at any given time—in Rochester. We badly needed more space and my grandfather wanted to help. He agreed to give my mom and dad his home on Reliance Street for free if they took over the $5,000 mortgage.

The house was compact, maybe 1,200 square feet, with three bedrooms. I shared a room with my sister, Marie, and little brother, Emil. My sister, Anna , had a small room to herself. We all shared one bathroom that had only a tiny sink, toilet, and tub. There was no shower. I was about five when we moved and it seemed okay to me, coal furnace and all. I didn't even know what air conditioning was.

During the Depression, everyone needed coal so my grandfather always had work. By the 1950s he owned a big truck that he parked in the garage at our house. We kids sometimes got to ride in it with him, and it was great fun for all of us.

I remember growing up that I needed to pay attention to the furnace, so I would often go down and shovel coal into the furnace and then shovel out the ashes a few times a week. By the 1950s most people had central heating, but we always had a coal furnace. We had a large coal bin in the basement right next to the furnace to store the coal as needed.

On Saturday mornings I would go with my mother to the Rochester Community War Memorial where they would distribute large boxes of food to qualified families. We qualified. The boxes contained big cans of peanut butter, large square blocks of American cheese, and cans of soup and sauce.

My Aunt Anna and Uncle Horace moved to Buffalo and thanks to my uncle's company, Gioia Macaroni, they were quite well off. Every few months a Gioia truck would pull up to our house and deliver boxes of spaghetti and cans of Gioia sauce. Sometimes there might be a box of clothes that my aunt's seven children no longer needed. I didn't know these cousins very well. They were rich by any standard I knew, and, to me, they lived in another world. I am now quite close to all of them.

When I think back I realize we lived in a place where we did not belong. We could never have afforded to buy a home in that neighborhood and we could hardly afford to live there. My parents remortgaged the house several times to take a little money out. The mortgage was never paid off until the house was sold in 1975. On some level I think I knew all of this and I resented everyone for it. It broke my heart to see my mother struggle to put even the simplest meals on the table. She would make a large pot of sauce on Sunday and it stayed on the stove all week for meals of pasta and whatever meat she could throw in there—meatballs were typical. I can still see her counting out the nickels and dimes until I had enough to buy a hot dog with my friends. She was cutting into the family budget because she knew how much I wanted that special treat.

I began to swim competitively at the YMCA when I was in the seventh grade. It turned out I was pretty good at the breaststroke and I began to win some races. My mother was at every meet and I remember hearing her cheer me on even while I was in the water.

By the time I started high school at Ben Franklin in 1964 I had developed into a pretty good swimmer, winning local and statewide competitions. I loved winning and it made me feel good that my mother was so proud of me. Plus, it didn't cost anything, so it was good all around.

In high school I was enlisted to join the varsity team my freshman year, but the team already had the best breaststroker in town; he had set the city record. So I was a backup to some big stars. But then they graduated and In my sophomore year I became city champ in the 100 yard breaststroke and a member of our school's champion medley relay team. My mother was busting out all over. It made me happy to be able to give her a little joy. My father never came to see me swim. But I knew he was aware of it and he saw my picture in the paper. He was proud of me but never said a word.

I was always a good, hardworking, tough kid, and a loyal friend, too. Older guys always liked having me around when I was young because I was tough and strong for my age. Once, when I was in the fifth or sixth grade, four brothers Who lived nearby, and were sort of frineds of mine, were walking home with me for lunch. We actually walked to and from school, up a big hill, every day. Earlier that day my mother had yelled at them for riding their bikes through her hanging laundry so that she had to wash the sheets again. On our lunchtime walk the four of them told me they had formed a club: The DiNardo Haters. I felt a switch go off in my head. So I asked what the club did and they said if any DiNardo said or did anything bad to one of them that they all would respond together. I blanked out and went into fight mode against all four brothers. At some point as I was wrestling with one of them another one came running in with a large tree branch and broke it over my back. I charged him and had him pinned to the sidewalk and began to pound his head into the cement.

Thankfully, some garbage men saw the whole thing and came running and pulled me off saying, "Whoa, hold on little guy, you could kill him." They said they had seen what happened but that I needed to calm down. The brothers ran off. I was crying and the garbage men continued to hold me. I felt I had been fighting for my mother and protecting the family name. I was all mixed up but eventually I calmed down and went home. The brothers disbanded the club. We were sort of friends again. But not really.

Every now and then the remnant of that suppressed anger pops up for a moment. I have worked hard to gain some insight into this part of my youth. When I was hurt or angry, I often found myself alone in my bedroom. I remember thinking that if I could just focus on a pinpoint in my mind, one tiny little thing, I could somehow be in a place separate from all these powerful feelings. Looking back, I find that so interesting, given my strong attraction to meditation and mindfulness practices. Even before I had the formal knowledge, or the language to articulate my feelings, I already seemed to understand a lot about what it meant to seek within.

Getting a Start

I was not a good student in high school. My average was about a 76, no better. But because of Maxine, my girlfriend at the time, I applied to Brockport, a small state school, and was accepted. I ended up doing so well that I was able to transfer to SUNY Buffalo, where I was later accepted to law school. Since no one in my family had even gone to college, this was quite an accomplishment.

When I first became an attorney I was still a bit of a radical at heart. I looked the part, too: I had a beard and long hair that I wore in a ponytail. But when I began to represent my clients in court, I soon realized that what I was doing was important to the people I represented and that I should do everything to help them. Being in court completely changed my view of life, the legal system, and the impact both could have on those that were the least able to speak for themselves. Eventually I realized my appearance was getting in the way of my helping my clients.

So one Saturday I cut my hair and shaved and I loved what I saw. I had only one suit and no shoes, only a pair of clogs but, man, could I talk and make a cogent argument. Lawyers liked me and appreciated my working class background. They soon realized that I really loved my clients and worked hard to help them. I did everything. Divorces, criminal, a little bankruptcy if necessary. Mostly I loved being in court and speaking or actually trying a case.

The first criminal case I had was a DWI in the town of Hamburg, a middle class suburb of Buffalo. My boss said he would meet me in court and show me how to try a case, pick a jury, and make objections. He never showed up and I had to do it alone; I felt like I was flying by the seat of my pants. I did it anyway. I made some mistakes, but I think the jury, the judge, and even the prosecutor liked me for being able to pull it all off. Even if I hadn't played by all the rules, I still won.

In a year or so my boss and I realized that we needed to focus more on making money and that seeking out personal injury cases was a good way to do this. I tried many cases and began to make a name for myself, and we soon began to do really well. I started making money and met Stephanie; we married in 1978. I was almost 32 and she was 28. The wedding was at my cousin's house in Buffalo and afterwards we went to my retreat outside the city. It was a small, private six-acre lakeside spot with three cabins; my law partner, John F. Collins, and I had received the land and cabins in exchange for doing legal work for the farmer that built them.

Stephanie had an MSW and she began a small private practice that soon began to grow. Kids were not on our radar yet and we had some bumpy times. We even split up for a year or so between 1983 and 1984. When we got back together, we decided to have a child, but Stephanie could not get pregnant, so in 1990, we adopted Josh, a beautiful baby boy. At first, adopting felt strange. But one night, when Josh was about six months old, I was rocking him in his room in the dim light. Suddenly I was overcome with a deep feeling of unconditional love for him and a sense of the responsibility I had taken on. I whispered to him, "Josh, I will always love you and be here for you no matter what may come." That feeling never went away and I never felt "strange" about adopting again.

In the early 1990s my family-owned law firm began to experience some bad times and it split up into two factions. I was overcome with grief and could not believe what was happening. Eventually I had to see that it was a treacherous environment and that I had to accept the inevitable changes that were being forced upon me.

Stephanie was not used to this kind of environment and we had very different ideas about how I should handle the problems at work. I felt like I was fighting on two fronts: at the office and at home. Soon we realized I needed to move out for a time.

Our marriage didn't survive. We parted amicably, and I gave her everything I had, willing to start afresh.

Soon after our divorce, I began to phone-flirt with Marcia. We made our first visit together to New York City in 1993 and were always together after that. By 1997 she had formed a strong bond with my son, Josh, who was seven, and Marcia and I married on May 1, 1999.

Finding the Buddhist Way

Back in 1973, I was renting a small one-bedroom apartment on the corner of Elmwood and Virginia in Buffalo. There was a group of mostly elderly folks that seemed to use the one large room that made up much of the first floor. They met every Friday and all of them seemed sweet and gentle. I was curious about the group so I asked about the substance of their meetings. They said they were all members of the Theosophical Society, a worldwide non-religious organization Mostly inclined to Buddhism but open to all theologies. Each week one member gave a talk on one subject of their choosing. I went to a few meetings, and I liked them. I read about the Founder, Madame Blavatsky, and her child protectorate, Krishnamurti. Many years later I was able to hear Krishnamurti in Calcutta give a wonderful talk for free.

After a few meetings I agreed to give a talk on Buddhism and began to read and research. I was hooked. Buddhism spoke my language. "I get it," was what I thought, and I began to meditate and to experience some of what I had read and thought I understood. Around the same time I read a book called *Be Here Now* by Ram Dass, formerly known as Dr. Richard Alpert, Ph.D. from Harvard, and Timothy Leary, his partner. I soon contacted Ram Dass and arranged a weekend retreat with him as my star attraction. Two hundred meditators showed up, and it was incredible. At the end of the weekend, Ram Dass told me about some friends that had spent years in India and southeast Asia studying and practicing Buddhist meditation. That very fall they were opening a new meditation center, Insight Meditation Society (IMS) in Barre, Massachusetts, and he wanted me to go for one week every month for four months until I came for four full weeks.

Before this, I had no real experience of what mindfulness practice was all about and no idea about how transformative it could be. But my first week of silence and meditation was a revelation. The idea that everything is in flux, nothing is permanent, and all is changing resonated deeply with me. Meditation showed me that there are no real places to "take a stand." It was better to be "in the stream," moving with the flow rather than clinging to branches, trying to fight the current. Real peace and liberation has come from surrendering control and cultivating the ability to watch and observe the mind as it unfolds. Being in the moment is not some lofty, mystery-shrouded plane of existence. Instead, it is simply focusing on the moment as it is unfolding, without adding to it or taking anything away.

It is through Buddhist practice that something quite profound happens and we begin to develop the wisdom to see things as they are and the compassion to love and accept others as they are. We are all just doing the best we can at any given moment.

This struck a chord when I was first introduced to it, and made sense to me both intellectually and experientially. Just the simple act of slowly moving toward and then reaching for a doorknob. Touching, feeling, turning, pushing. What a wonderful process. And as I slowed down and watched, I saw all of the constant, automatic recordings I continued to play in my head. My auto response, so to speak, rather than being fully present. Awake. It was that mindset that allowed me to see the weaknesses in my marriage and to accept that the marriage was not strong enough to make it through what was to be a long and difficult legal battle with my former partners.

This was my entrance into Buddhism, more than 40 years ago, and my Buddhist practice has proven to be a central part of my life. Buddhism was with me when I was slapped with a diagnosis of a large brain tumor and facing my own mortality. And Buddhism helped me so much in the two years following Marcia's diagnosis in February of 2013. Buddhism gave me a way to understand my own life, and a way to live it fully and deeply.

A Baby Girl

After Marcia and I had been together for eight years, we married and decided we wanted to have a child. But we were unable to conceive. We tried in vitro fertilization, but that did not work, so we decided to adopt. My son, Josh, was adopted, so that was cool with me—and Marcia was all for it.

So, in 2000, we began to pursue private adoption in New York state. We soon found a married woman with two sons who found herself unexpectedly pregnant. She and her husband had agreed they were not in an emotional or financial position to care for another child. There had been another interested couple from Chicago, but that fell through. The way was open for us.

Marcia and I were on a ski slope in Aspen when I received the call. Marcia began to weep with joy—we might be having a baby girl soon. The baby was due in early May, so we made sure everything was good with the prospective mother and the legal situation, and then we went off on a long-planned trip to Rome that began on Easter Saturday. Our attorney had assured us that it was okay.

We arrived in Rome early Saturday morning and checked into our hotel near the Spanish Steps. All good. I decided to call our attorney and just check in as we were both getting a little excited as the due date approached. I got her on the phone and was shocked to hear that the birth mother was in labor at Sisters Hospital and "our" baby girl had decided to enter the world a few weeks early. We called the concierge to get us any flight he could back home, only to be told, "This is Easter weekend in Rome, Italy. You're not going *anywhere* for a few days."

We soon learned that we would need to wait until the birth mother actually checked out and went home alone, without our daughter, in order for us to pick the baby up. The problem was that the baby was born Saturday night and the mother was scheduled to leave the hospital Monday morning. We were stranded in Rome until who knew when! Finally, we made arrangements to get a Monday night flight that would arrive in Toronto on Tuesday. Marcia's sister, Marie, was quickly designated by the surrogate judge (who was a close friend and mentor to me) as guardian until we could return home, as the hospital was insisting the baby leave Monday night or they would deliver her to family services. Marie picked up our precious baby girl and waited for our arrival the next day. It had all worked and, amazingly, the baby was ours.

While we waited in Rome we debated a name. Marcia suggested Marianna or Julianna, which was her favorite. I suggested Bertha after my mother but, sentiment aside, Marcia was very opposed to it. As we were leaving we stopped to thank the concierge for his help. I speak reasonable Italian so I asked his opinion on the names. When he heard all three choices He first said, in his most elegant Italian, "Eh, Bertha e brutta!" or, "Bertha is ugly!" We all laughed. So Bertha was out. And it turned out his mother was named Julianna. Marcia was smiling—she took it as a sign from heaven—and the naming procedure was over. Our baby girl was to be named Julianna. We chose Marie as a middle name, to honor Marcia's sister who had stepped in to save the day.

Julianna Marie DiNardo (JMD) became our treasure. We loved and adored her, and doted upon her in so many ways, both great and small. But soon we began to notice small things. One eye drifted and needed small surgery for repair. And as she began to walk we noticed that her coordination seemed somehow a little off. She had difficulty running. At four and five she was extremely shy. We tried to get her some help and were told shyness was a gene and often a child grows out of it. She certainly has improved, although she is still shy.

Once she began attending school it was clear that she had challenges in learning to read and to do math, and she rebelled at having to learn these things that frustrated her so. She was also very shy, and not well coordinated. She always tried to be like everyone else but it was very hard. I like to say her best friend, Hayley, is 15 going On 20, and Julianna is 15 going on 12. But, oh, how Marcia loved, guided, and protected her. She never judged her, but accepted her fully for who she is. As soon as she realized the extent of Julianna's issues, she clicked into high mother mode, and worked hard to address them. She knew Julianna needed friends, and so made sure that other kids entered Julianna's world.

Marcia often said to me, "I know why I'm here. It is to take care of Julianna. That is my purpose in life." Julianna needed her desperately. I loved to watch those two interact. You could almost touch the love and bond they shared. And there is nothing like the love and relationship between a mother and a daughter. It is truly a thing of beauty.

Then the news. When I told Julianna about her mother's diagnosis, it seemed as if she was not wired to understand the gravitas of the situation. That was often the case with her, so I was not surprised. But I wanted her to understand as best she could how sick her mom was and how difficult the battle was going to be. These days, Julianna is complicated and difficult to read. She was deeply affected by Marcia's death. She was very close to her mother and relied on her for emotional support. I know that learning to accept this loss will be one of the great challenges in her life.

The Worst News

Sometime in late February 2013 I was away on a business trip, and when I called to Check-in with Marcia she said she was having stomach trouble. It "felt hard," she said. The sensation continued into the next day, when she also complained of a rash and began scratching all the time. Yet neither of us were particularly alarmed.

But when I got home, I saw that Marcia was turning yellow, a sure sign of jaundice, and I knew she needed to see a doctor. I made the call and we were told to consult a gastrointestinal doctor who specialized in abdominal problems. The specialist was able to see her that day and he diagnosed gallstones, and mentioned the possibility of other gallbladder issues. The doctor said Marcia might need a stent to open any blocked ducts, but first she would need to have a scope, a procedure that took about 40 minutes. The scope, we were told, would find any stones and remove them. It was even able to insert a stent. If her gallbladder needed to come out, the surgeon would perform that operation the following day. She would be home shortly after. This all made sense to both of us, and once Marcia was given medication, she was able to tolerate the discomfort.

Marcia and I went to Buffalo General early on a Saturday morning, where we heard the same information we'd already heard. Marcia went in for the short scope procedure. I sat in the small waiting room where time seemed to tick as if in slow motion. After an hour-and-a-half they began to close the waiting room for the weekend. I began to get concerned but figured it was a hospital and they must have been backed up.

After I had been sitting for about two hours in the now darkened waiting room, the doctor performing Marcia's procedure, whom I did not know, came out to see me. "Joe, sorry it took so long, but when we went in we did not see any stones at all. So we kept looking. I looked at the gallbladder, and it's also fine. But something is blocking this duct in the pancreas. We put in a stent so she'll feel pretty good once the fluids that were all backed up begin to flow." I asked what was blocking it in the first place. His response was, "You should talk to her gastroenterologist," someone we also did not know.

I was puzzled. "You're a doctor," I said, "Why don't you just tell me what you think?"

"Well, I thought it might be a very large stone that got away but I scraped and pushed at it and yet I still couldn't find it. I have been doing this for 30 years and I don't think it is a stone at all. Please wait to speak to your doctor later today." He sounded very uncomfortable and it was clear he did not want to pursue this conversation with me. "Marcia will be going back to her room soon. I think you should spend the night here with her."

With that he was gone, never to be seen again. We soon went to her room and patiently waited for "our" doctor to call. Finally, around 7:30 p.m., he called my cell and I put it on speaker so Marcia could hear.

"I know you've spoken to the doctor who did the scope," he began. "I've confirmed with him that there are no gallstones. Marcia's gallbladder is fine. The stent should make her feel better."

"She is feeling better," I said, "But if she doesn't have gallstones, what does she have?"

"I can't help you." He sounded nervous. "I cannot help you anymore."

I thought this was an odd answer and I said, "Okay, but can't you at least tell me what you think the problem is?"

"You need to change your treatment options." Again, odd. "I think you need to think about Roswell." I knew perfectly well that Roswell was a cancer hospital.

"Are you saying there's something on my wife's pancreas blocking the duct? A growth?"

"Yes. You need to get to Roswell. She has a growth on her pancreas."

I was looking at Marcia. Her face registered fear, confusion, and anxiety. I hung up and in that instant I had such an extraordinary experience it is difficult to explain. I knew with utter certainty that no matter what happened, I was committed to being with her every step of the way on this new and frightening journey. And, for the first time in my life, I was completely infused with an all-encompassing love for her. A feeling of love so deep that it needed nothing in return. All of this occurred in a flash but I felt it to my core.

I continued to look at Marcia. She was shaken, though she was clearly not quite sure what she had heard. "Why Roswell?" she asked.

"Honey, I'm not sure, so let's take it one step at a time." I knew this was bad. I was not sure how much Marcia understood but, until we got to Roswell, I wasn't going to start guessing about that or anything else. I only assured her that whatever this was we would face it together. And that I loved her unconditionally. But really, we were both scared.

In a few days Marcia was settled at Roswell. It was a wonderful facility where the staff created a soft place for people to land when dealing with the most difficult issues possible. The scans showed a growth on her pancreas and nothing else. The surgeon explained that it would be possible to do surgery *if* the growth was confined to this single location. While complicated, the procedure provided patients with pancreatic cancer a real chance of survival if done early enough. That meant before it had metastasized or migrated somewhere else.

Ouch! It was the first time the c-word had been used. It hurt and I could feel Marcia stiffen in response. After all was explained he said, "Oh, I should mention. We saw a little lesion, or shadow, on the liver. Very small and I doubt it's anything. Not unusual. But when she goes in for the surgery we'll biopsy it first. If it is cancer, and it has spread, we can't do the surgery at all."

We left stunned by this entire shift in our lives. While we both always agreed that life can always bring new and unexpected twists, neither of us was remotely prepared for this. There was fear, of course. Confusion everywhere. We had no concrete answers, only more questions. Of course all our family and friends wanted to know everything at once. But we didn't know anything, so I began to research—to call friends, doctors, and a very close friend whose wife had died of pancreatic cancer five years earlier.

I made arrangements to visit Memorial Sloan Kettering Cancer Center in New York City and we sent them all the scans and hospital records to date. They were ready for us. The surgeon, Dr. Paul Allen, gave us confidence: he had performed many of these operations, and he felt he could do Marcia's, too. "Oh, yes, and one more thing," he said. "There was this little spot. A shadow, really."

We had heard this before. And he did not think it was anything, either. He wanted Marcia to take medication to shrink everything prior to surgery. Then he said, "Go on your vacation and come back ready for pre-op. We'll do a biopsy of that little spot prior to surgery, just to be sure." He said his top radiologist would be looking at the scans over the weekend. So we left for Florida with our daughter Julianna and some other family members.

On Monday morning in Florida my cell phone rang. It was Dr. Allen from Sloan Kettering. He said that we needed to get that little shadow biopsied before pre-op. In fact, we needed to get it done as soon as possible.

"Why?" I asked. "What did your top radiologist say that changed your mind?"

"Well, it may be something and we really need confirmation. It's very small but we have an incredibly gifted doctor and she assures me she'll get enough for a biopsy. When can you get here?" I could tell he was being deliberately vague because we were on the phone, and Marcia and I were on vacation, but I also sensed that he wanted to be truthful with us.

Marcia was just beginning to get her feet under her after all that had happened, and I knew that this change in plan would only turn up the heat. I saw that she was scared, confused, and disheartened. But I also saw a certain steely resolve set in. She did not want to be a victim or even a patient. She wanted to be a fighter.

My heart had started to crumble as any last sense of real hope was being slowly stripped away. What to do? *Be with it, Joe, feel it, see it, let the answer just come, don't force it.* That's what I told myself. This was all new territory for me and the stakes were getting higher than anything I had ever expected or experienced.

We returned to Memorial Sloan Kettering a few days later, nervous and apprehensive about the results of the biopsy. We were shuttled into a large office where Dr. Allen, the surgeon, soon arrived, along with four young doctors-in-training. Dr. Allen sat down and said, "I guess we should discuss the biopsy first." We smiled nervously and Marcia squeezed my hand. "It was positive for cancer," he said. "Surgery is out of the question. Now that the disease has metastasized, it would be malpractice to operate. Too dangerous."

I asked what this meant for her diagnosis and he replied, "It goes from a stage I to stage IV." I knew what that meant. My stomach lurched and the thoughts began to whirl in my head. Could this really be happening? Could I really be losing her? What does she need from me? How do we even get home?

I was paralyzed. The doctors told us that Marcia would benefit most from chemo and radiation and that Roswell was as good as anyplace to do it. Plus we would be home. A small flicker in a very long, dark tunnel. I turned to Marcia.

"We'll be home, honey, where I can best take care of you. We'll have Erin and Mona and your mom and whole family. We can do this. You're young and strong and there are no rules now. I will find everything possible to help you fight this."

Somehow we made it back to Buffalo. Tears everywhere. Family, friends everyone, shocked and shattered. Not possible. Not to Marcia. No, no, *no way*. But there it was, the 800-pound gorilla, sitting at the head of the table. We could not avoid what was about to unfold.

We really didn't know what to expect from the chemo. It was just so hard to even believe this was happening to my baby. But we began. We arrived at Roswell within days of getting back home. Roswell was not like any regular hospital you might imagine. It was full of light, and live jazz or live classical music was played in all the common areas. People smiled, even those who were so obviously ill. Everyone was warm and friendly. This was a space cultivated with warmth and love. Every patient here was battling cancer. It was everywhere.

We arrived at our room and soon it all began. Marcia was hooked up and the drugs began to flow into her veins. I wanted to puke right there and could only imagine what Marcia was feeling and thinking. Not knowing what was happening or how it was going to happen, I began to feel like I was breaking apart. I could do nothing to take away her fear and pain. Nothing. And with time it only got worse.

It was hard at first for me. Knowing what I knew of the disease, I did not know how to be for Marcia. During her second chemo session, Chris Diamantis, my business partner, and I followed Dr. Iyer out into the hall and I asked her to be honest with me. Dr. Iyer was the oncologist and she was soon to become my ocean of compassion.

Dr. Iyer said that it was fairly typical with a stage IV diagnosis that patients might live six months or so. If she made it twelve months, it would be considered a good result, and anything more would be very unusual. But she ended by telling me, "Joe we can never take away her hope. Listen, and you'll hear what she wants to know and when she wants to know it. It's not our job to steal her hope—that's all she has."

What profound advice. And so I began the process of listening to Marcia, trying to go beyond the façade or show. I learned to judge her willingness to hear my thoughts and just how much she really wanted to know. I also recommitted myself to my mindfulness practice. To stay in the moment as much as possible. To be with all my insecurities and fears and not try to change them or distract myself from feeling them in all their power. As I did that more and more, the power those negative thoughts had over me diminished and the space that was created allowed me to be more fully present for my wife.

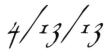

4/13/13

Again, thank you all for your continued support and outpouring of love.

Marcia had her second chemo treatment yesterday. They drew blood first and we then met w Dr. Iyer (who is absolutely fabulous). Somehow some way Marcia's white blood count had actually risen. It is expected to decrease from the chemo and that reduces your immune system and subjects you to greater risk of other diseases causing sickness etc. She really shocked the doctor w that result. Maybe it is all the new supplements she is taking or the acupuncture or all the prayers that are being said for her. Not important why but just so comforting that she had that finding.

We found a Tibetan-trained physician in Amherst that is licensed in acupuncture. Very sweet and has 30 years of experience. Dr. May Wang. The acupuncture may help decrease the side effects of the chemo. The fatigue, nausea, headaches, and general feeling of sickness. Marcia is going to see her several times a week. We are also seeing a Qigong practitioner in Buffalo as it is too difficult to travel to NYC to see Robert Peng. We will still see him as her condition allows us to travel some. It is all a little crazy but the stakes are just too high not to pursue alternate types of treatments as well as the chemo.

She was very weak last night and I expect her to be quite fatigued for a few days as she also has the continuous chemo drip attached to her for 2 more days.

I already love and respect her so much but she has been such a wonderful and courageous person that I am truly more amazed at how gracefully she is handling all of this. As you know the diagnosis is still very harsh but Marcia is convinced she is going to beat this and she has made a believer out of me.

THANK YOU ALL SO MUCH. WORDS CANNOT CONVEY HOW MUCH ALL YOUR SUPPORT HAS HELPED MARCIA EACH DAY

Joe

The first eight rounds of chemotherapy took about 16 weeks. Marcia did very well. Actually, the doctors could not believe that her cancer marker shrank to almost 45. Normal is considered 35 or so. We felt blessed and began to think, even believe, that she might be the one to beat all the odds. The one the doctors tell stories about to those searching for any ray of hope in an otherwise hopeless situation.

But like the saying, what goes up must come down and as high as our hopes climbed it was not long before they were dashed again. After the 16 weeks of chemo, she had a two-week break, and then a month of radiation. Following the radiation, there was another CT scan and it was then that we learned her cancer had now lodged on to the other side of the liver, and elsewhere. Her markers skyrocketed. More radiation treatments followed. It was somewhat helpful. The process, once again, shrank some of the tumors—but not all. More chemo was all they had, so chemo was what they used to battle the cancer.

11/3/14

So much has been happening that it did not seem possible to write anything that might change before u even read it. So, sparing u all the nitty-gritty details, it has been a bit of a roller coaster ride. Marcia's cancer marker went down then suddenly began a steep climb and ultimately hit 6400 when it had been as low as 45. We were quite disheartened and confused. Marcia was in the middle of the vaccine clinical trial and also on chemo. She switched chemo which was good but unfortunately it caused her to lose all her hair. And we also learned that the vaccine needed to be front end loaded before they expect any real benefit. Well the benefit began as the marker dropped from 6400 to 2300 almost overnight and then stabilized there for a few weeks. Today was another chemo day and the marker has again dropped to 1605. So that is significant and the fact that it is "trending" down is very good. Much of this may also be due to the new chemo as well.

Her spirit and resolve and strength through all of this has been unfaltering and, frankly, inspiring, at least to me. I see the toll the chemo takes physically and emotionally and psychologically, now for 21 months. We are hoping that very soon she can get a break from the chemo for a good period of time and maybe a long period if the vaccine therapy is successful.

We have traveled to Italy and France this summer. We have spent time w the closest of friends in the Hamptons and shared time w loving family and friends often. She loves it and she loves that all of u keep her in your thoughts, prayers, meditations, and heart. She is off the charts as far as the doctors are concerned and she defies all the standards one might usually expect in this situation. I am honored to be her husband and friend.

Thanks again,
Joe

⌒

Eighteen months into the treatment, a clinical trial of a new vaccine came along. First they cleansed the blood in Marcia's entire body. Then they actually took her cancer cells and used them to make a vaccine only for her. Unlike chemo, the vaccine would attack only the cancer cells and nothing else. It was very complicated and there was no proof it would work. It didn't, though her doctors were pleased because they were able to extend her life by a few months.

At that point, there really were no good options. I told the medical staff that the chemo was not working except to destroy her and make her sicker, if that was even possible. I told Dr. Iyer that we should stop the chemo, and shift our attention to pain management and quality of life issues.

Marcia had very much wanted to take a trip to Anguilla that we had planned, and so we did that. And during Julianna's spring break we went to Naples, Florida, another place Marcia wanted to go. But we had to cut the trip short and come home early because she was so sick.

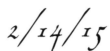

$2/14/15$

Been a while since my last report and sorry for such a long pause. Much has occurred and sometimes our heads just spin w the speed and overwhelming issues that come up.

Marcia has lost a considerable amount of weight and is now on a 12 hour TPN nutrition drip to try and get her immune system back up and fighting.

There is new cancer in and around the duodenum, which is problematic, and at the moment not able to treat due to her inability to deal w any more chemo. Difficult but not impossible and her courage and spirit remain strong.

We are going to spend a week w her entire family in Florida now during school break and then home to continue on the vaccine protocol. Your prayers, loving kindness, and support remain the bedrock of her strength and for that we thank you one and all.

For the last three days of her life, Marcia was in bed, barely conscious, with her eyes closed. On one of those nights, I climbed into bed with her. She was hooked up to a catheter and an IV for the pain medications. She tore off her clothes and kept trying to get out of bed, and I kept gently restraining her.

On the morning of March 3, 2015 I phoned the hospice nurse in great distress. She offered to stop by that day, and she came over around 4:00 p.m. We went up to the bedroom together and then I left the room. When she came out, she said, "Joe, her blood pressure is non-existent but her heart is beating very hard to compensate. You should call the family and have them come; I don't think she'll make it through the night."

So that is what I did. All the tubes came out. Julianna climbed into bed with her, to say good-bye. As weak as she was, Marcia turned over and with her impossibly thin arms, hugged her daughter for a few seconds before letting go. Her mother, sisters, and brothers all had a chance to hold her hand and say a few words.

I sent Julianna out of the room while I waited for the end. Her lips curled a little and her soft breathing turned to gasps; this lasted about 30 seconds. Then she took her last breath. Her eyes opened (the nurse had told me this might happen) and I closed them. My Marcia was gone.

The Six-Month Mark

My love, it has been six months now since you left me. I thought it would get easier but in so many ways it is harder. At first the thought of you as gone forever was hard to accept. I kept thinking you would walk down the stairs to the kitchen for coffee as I sat waiting for you. But with time it has become so clear that you really are gone—forever. I miss you so much. Julianna needs you so much. I am a poor substitute for all the love and guidance with which you provided her. Your family has been wonderful and they help a great deal. But our daughter is 15 and, in addition to all the challenges she faces, she is at that age that is so awkward and dangerous. She bursts into fits of anger with me now like never before. You are not here to mitigate or comfort. She seems lost, but I am lost as well. She and Hayley still like dressing up in your clothes, and I love it when they do. Your mother and sisters and Erin have each a few pieces, too, but the closet is still full. What should I do?

I saw an old friend at the airport this week and she asked, "Are you seeing anyone yet?" By the look on my face she knew instantly that it was an inappropriate question. Was it? I said that I was not in that space yet. Not sure what that means, or if I ever will be. I don't even know what "that space" is for sure. It has been three full years since I was able to hold you in a full embrace. To kiss you. To make love to you. It was not and is not really a big deal, but I miss it so much. The warmth and safety of our bed.

I know now you are not ever going to come down those stairs again. And that is what I am adjusting to. I do not think I will heal with time. But I will adjust to this pain. Accept it more fully. Be with it and honor the feeling as it comes and goes. If I hurt so much it is because I was privileged to have loved so much. Thank you for giving me that.

Tonight was a marvelous, wonderful end to a sunny, beautiful, fall day in Buffalo. Since Julianna went to the Bills' home game at 9:00 in the morning, I spent the day alone. I sat out back, looking over the magnificent landscaping and backyard that you cultivated and designed. I felt guilty that I could be here experiencing all of this and you could not.

I missed you so, and the tears fell freely and endlessly. It was only the breeze, the sun, me—and all you had built. I could feel you everywhere and all over me, Marcia. Is it true that you are never coming back? Never? Six months and the loss feels as sharp now as it did then.

Life After Death

I don't know what happens when someone dies. I don't believe that life ends, that it's just over. Instead, what makes sense to me is this: we transition from here to somewhere that is a familiar space. We reside here for a time as we adjust to having to leave the world behind. The transition may be brief, or it may take a long time. I am not sure how time unfolds in that other realm. So now, each day, each night, each morning, I send you *metta* (loving kindness) to help in wherever your journey takes you, Marcia. I love you so much and miss you too much. But you know this. I still can't believe you're gone forever.

Grief and Time

I do not believe that time heals all wounds. It may heal some but not all. Certainly not the complete loss of someone you loved so hard and were loved deeply by in return. But time seems to allow one to adjust better to the loss. To incorporate it into life more fully. To honor the feelings surrounding the loss and to, almost, become friends with them. They arise out of nowhere and at the oddest times, when least expected. And there you are again and my heart stops and my stomach tightens and sadness seems to permeate my entire body. I have learned to pay more attention when these emotions arise. Not to push them away so fast. And then to carry on. No other choice. Although I now choose to be alone more because I am often not fit for normal discourse.

The other day it hit me so hard out of nowhere. I was in the office and suddenly: fatigue, sadness, lost, and the urgent need to go home. To our home. I did, and went into our room and into our bed, where I covered my head with a pillow and wept, sobbed and screamed. Then nothing. Sleep or something like sleep took over me. When I woke up I felt rested and the weight of my grief, the holidays, Julianna, and life seemed lighter—at least for the moment.

What I shared with Marcia was not perfect by any means. But for me it was perfectly imperfect and it worked. Our being together made me happy every day. Now as Julianna and I share pre-made salads from Wegmans or she eats frozen chicken fingers, I wonder if I told her enough how I appreciated the meals she made with such love for all of us and the joy she seemed to get from our pleasure consuming them. I wish I could thank her right now.

Julianna and I are back in Punta Mita, Mexico with Chris and family. He toasted you last night, and all the kids and some of the adults had a shot of tequila in your honor. Sweet, but I could not say anything because if I did, I knew the dam would break and tears would fall and I would have ruined the night and the toast.

Julianna loves being with Maggie (Chris's niece) and the girls and they take great care of her. She seems to have softened with me somewhat. I hope so. She so needs a soft place to fall and that place was always you. Life is such a challenge for her. She needs me and doesn't know it yet. Somehow we will get her through high school, but then what? I don't know what her future will hold.

Acceptance, Not Denial

Loss, grief, and despair are strong and overpowering emotional states that can linger. Most often, in the west, we work hard to get rid of these feelings as best we can. To hold them at bay, to get over them and convince ourselves that time heals all. But in my meditation practice I look at my grief and loss and acknowledge them. I allow myself to feel them deeply without trying to interfere with them or push them away. I am not trying to control them or to get over them at an appropriate time. By sitting with them in my daily meditations and acknowledging them through all my waking hours, I can watch my emotions as they unfold. Yes, my grief and sorrow over the loss of Marcia are overwhelming, but I am not overwhelmed. I feel it all so deeply. But in watching this and simply allowing it to *be*, I do not add any energy to the feelings and they are not artificially enhanced by me. The pain is real but I befriend it and accept it. This is a great opportunity for awakening for me. I loved and love Marcia so deeply, yet I believe that this loss is a privilege she has shared with me as neither of us had any control over the course of her illness and death. As we never do.

By recognizing that I have no real control over what occurs in life and what life presents to me, I then recognize that all I can control is how I respond. If I keep pushing away those things I do not like and keep clinging to the things I do like, I just keep the wheel going round and round. But if I can sit quietly and in stillness and simply allow events and feelings to unfold without trying to control everything, there is great relief from the additional stress that fighting these feelings brings to our lives. At least that is how it works for me.

My losses have been as great as my successes. I feel them deeply. Gradually. But I try not to push them away or to cling to them either. There is a great sense of humility in this for me, and also I feel the growth of compassion as I realize that I am just like everyone else. Quieting the mind and developing our ability to just *be* can be a very beautiful process.

Deepak Chopra says quieting the mind allows the wisdom and compassion to simply unfold. If you are in a dark room and simply open the shutters, the light will fill that room all by itself. Nothing else needs to be done. Just open the shutters. It is the same for us. Simply quiet the mind and the light will come in.

Chopra also talks about his idea of God. Instead of a God who is a separate entity who created the universe, which is what many religions espouse, Chopra asks, what if God *became* the universe? If this were true, then every living creature, every object great or small, would contain a piece of God. We would be part of God, and God would be in us. I find this a very plausible explanation of the divine.

Lessons Learned

When I think back on the last three years of my life with Marcia, I see that there are lessons, some simple and some profound, that I would like to share.

- Never take away the patient's hope for survival and learn to support that hope.
- I was a skeptic when it came to the power of healing thoughts or sending love. Not anymore. I am convinced that the extended group of friends and family that kept Marcia in their prayers, thoughts, and daily meditations all somehow gave her that additional strength that traditional medicine cannot, and enabled her to carry on for as long as she did.
- Always listen to assess what and how much the patient is able to hear. Some things should be left to the medical professionals. Often our loved ones are looking for emotional support and love from us.
- Remain open. Let go of your ego and your needs. It will be rewarding and character-building and, ultimately, a very freeing experience.
- Take care of yourself. If you allow yourself to become over-stressed and let your own immune system weaken, then you cannot help the person you love. And if you get physically sick, that presents an even greater danger. A person undergoing treatment for cancer, especially with chemotherapy, has a very suppressed

immune system and cannot afford to be around anyone who is infectious. So love yourself and feel absolutely no guilt taking some alone time to decompress. Take supplements for adequate vitamin and nutritional support. Get enough sleep. Stay strong. Nobody can do it all alone. If you can, get a small support team of friends and relatives to help. It will be good for all of you.

- It is rarely the will that gives up first. Most often the body, our machine, is the first to break down. It quits from exhaustion and often just the relentless pounding of chemo and other treatments. This does not mean that the aggressive treatment is wrong. Only that it is difficult to endure. Often it leads to a cure, but not always, so choose wisely.

- Take five minutes each day for yourself. Sit quietly with eyes closed and tell yourself to relax, be happy, and be free from suffering. Give yourself some loving kindness and non-judgmental self-acceptance. Simple as that. None of us are perfect. But we can be perfectly imperfect. Accept yourself, just as you are.

- Always get a second opinion. Your primary doctor or cancer treatment center actually prefers this so that they do not carry the burden of diagnosis all alone. It will be important to you and your loved one to know that the diagnosis and treatment plan are right.

- The importance of family and friends cannot be overlooked or overstated.

- If there are things your loved one wants to do or say to people, let them do that. It is their life, not yours. Try never to impose your will unless they are doing something that could hurt them.

- I like the idea that God did not *create* the universe but just *became* the universe. He/She is everything and everywhere. We just need to be open to it. Thinking this way may be the most painful challenge you will ever endure, but it can also serve as an even greater opportunity for you to open and grow as a person and as a spiritual being.

- Ask questions of the oncologist, doctor, and the nurses. There are no dumb or bad questions. Professionals forget that not everyone understands what is happening or what the drugs are designed to do. Ask until you understand. Take notes or you will forget what you've been told.
- *Always* ask about the side effects of any prescribed treatment plan or medication.
- Never give up hope, but always know the worst may still happen.
- If or when it is over, do not be afraid to grieve in the way that you need to grieve and not the way other people think you should be grieving.
- Remember: You can do this.

Perhaps the greatest lesson I have learned is the one of humility with gratitude. When you are given the honor to care for someone you love unconditionally while she is suffering and dying in front of you, you begin to understand how small and insignificant your daily complaints are. Arthritic back, sore knee, common cold, broken bone. All of which we know will pass, even if we do nothing. But to watch a loved one suffer intractable pain and endure chemotherapy over the course of months is a humbling experience. At the same time, I also realized how truly grateful I am to be fully in this life and not to be suffering and dying.

If we allow ourselves to be open to all the suffering, pain, and helplessness we experience, something very powerful occurs. But we must put in the effort to *be* with the feelings and experiences. If we do this in a non-judgmental and open way, not only do we come closer to understanding what our loved one is actually experiencing, but we also deepen our senses of compassion and love. I made the effort to do this on a daily basis, during Marcia's chemo treatments, while she slept, when others visited with her. Rather than run from my sense of helplessness and panic at watching the end-of-life process, I stayed with it, watched it, and experienced it as best I could. I was rewarded silently with greater feelings of love and understanding, at least to some small degree, of what Marcia was going through. Being a caretaker, being with someone who is marching to an inevitable conclusion, is the most difficult thing you can do. Opening up to it rather than allowing our conditioned responses (trying to make it better or to go away) to take over allows us to grow and deepen our genuine love and compassion. At least that is how it has worked for me. Simply sit and let the feelings come, whatever they may be. Let them wash over you, make you cry, get angry or feel defeated. Just let it all happen inside without judgment or a response of any kind. It is natural, and everyone experiences these feelings—it is our human condition. If we watch we learn, in a way, that words do not seem adequate to provide.

I never truly appreciated how strong and what a warrior Marcia was until I saw how she handled her illness for two years before her body simply gave up. Her spirit never faltered but the machine simply could not do it anymore. She was a real hero who never complained. Sure, when we were alone in our room we would talk, and we each expressed our disbelief about how all of this could be happening. She made a bucket list. She organized her jewelry and handbags, each to be given to certain friends and family members. But she never talked about giving in and I never said anything to steal her hope of beating the disease. Watching her bravery, I learned some very good lessons about real strength and spirit.

A few days before the end, she sat up in bed. A skeleton. Beautiful. She asked, for the first time, "Do you think I'm going to get better?" She looked at me as I knelt on the floor. I knew she wanted the truth.

"No, my sweet, I don't think you are going to get better."

She paused, looked out the window and then back at me, and said, "Oh."

That was it.

Resources

Each of these individuals and institutions served Marcia and our family
with compassion, honesty, and expertise throughout her cancer journey.

Medical Resources

Peter J. Allen, MD, FACS
Memorial Sloan Kettering
1275 York Avenue
New York, NY 10065
800.525.2225
https://www.mskcc.org

Renuka Iyer, MD
Roswell Park Cancer Institute
646 Main Street
Buffalo, NY 14202
716.845.2300
https://www.roswellpark.org

Memorial Sloan Kettering
1275 York Avenue
New York, NY 10065
800.525.2225
https://www.mskcc.org

Robert Peng
RobertQigongSeminar@gmail.com

Roswell Park Cancer Institute
646 Main Street
Buffalo, NY 14202
716.845.2300
https://www.roswellpark.org

May Wang, MD
May Wang Medical Acupuncture
6511 Main Street
Williamsville, NY 14221
716.626.0102

Mindfulness Resources

Insight Meditation Society
1230 Pleasant Street
Barre, MA 01005
978.355.4378
https://www.dharma.org

When Things Fall Apart: Heart Advice for Difficult Times by Pema Chodron (1997)
Living Beautifully: with Uncertainty and Change, 2013 by Pema Chodron (2012)
Seeking the Heart of Wisdom: The Path of Insight Meditation by Joseph Goldstein and
    Jack Kornfield (1987)
The Experience of Insight: A Simple and Direct Guide to Buddhist Meditation by Joseph
    Goldstein (1976)

About the Author

Joseph DiNardo, Esq. is the CEO, director, and founder of Counsel Financial, a highly specialized commercial lender offering loans and credit lines to law firms. In these roles he oversees all business transactions and provides long-term strategy for the company.

Prior to founding Counsel Financial in 2000, Joe practiced mass tort and personal injury law for over 26 years. During his extensive trial career he represented thousands of injured plaintiffs, securing multi-million dollar, high-profile settlements or awards on cases tried to verdict.

Joe has lectured for the New York State and American Bar Associations as well as the New York State Trial Lawyers Association. He is a graduate of the State University of New York at Buffalo Law School and has been featured several times in *Best Lawyers in America*, the oldest and most respected peer-review publication in the legal profession.

A Letter to My Wife is Joe's first book, a labor of love dedicated to his late wife, Marcia

Made in the USA
Middletown, DE
20 November 2016